THE GENTLEMAN'S GUIDE
TO COOKING THROUGH A CHILD CUSTODY BATTLE

BY E.B. GUNN

Published by GunShy Press
email to: gsp@gentlemansguidetodivorce.com

www.gentlemansguidetodivorce.com

cover by: Maker
www.makerny.com

ISBN-10: 0985489227 (pod softcover)
ISBN-13: 978-0-9854892-2-9 (pod softcover)
first edition

<u>Disclaimer</u>
The characters and events portrayed in this book are amalgams drawn from the author's experience. Any similarity to individuals, living or dead, is purely coincidental and not intended by the author.

<u>Legal Notice</u>

For my bushwhacking buddies,

Scoop and Squirrel.

Together we climb mountains.

Table of Contents

Cooking for the kids

Cooking for ladyfriends

Appendices

<u>Preface</u>

"Well the first days are the hardest days…"
-Uncle John's Band-

Divorce brings with it many sudden shocks. A big one for guys is that it is very likely they will be pitched out of the family house and into a nearby house or apartment. I know a guy who went from, at least he thought, happily and monogamously married with a nanny cooking many of his meals and his wife cooking the rest, to out of the house, and seeing his kids on the weekends ... in 15 days. Always keep at least one friend who's a resourceful realtor in your network so in a pinch you can get a place. But then what?

Sure, my friend could go out to dinner or to his club every weeknight, but it looks pretty pathetic a guy kicked out of his house and sitting alone at dinner night after night. And the worst thing about looking pathetic is it makes you feel pathetic. His lawyer had quite correctly told him, as lawyers do, "No girls yet." And while he had many friends, there wasn't anybody he wanted to have dinner with mano-on-mano more than once a year. He was a guy. And he wanted to keep his kids. So what to do?

Easy. Well, maybe not easy. But with a little guidance, doable. To break old habits you'll have to trick yourself a little. Here's what I mean. You think cooking is a waste of time, but surfing the sports channels is time well spent, right? Okay, in the new crib set up the kitchen with a television so you can cook while you surf. Nobody likes doing the dishes, or emptying the dishwasher or straightening up the kitchen. But for you to succeed you will have to do these things, regularly. So get your favorite dancing music into the kitchen too. It is axiomatic that rhythm brings spark to drudgery. Just ask soldiers marching, the towel-snappers at the carwash, or the spinners at the spin class. So when it's time to clean, it's also time to rock. To win the fight to keep your kids, begin by making the new kitchen a hospitable place. You're going to be spending some time in there. Wire it.

7

Okay, let's get started. Here's how *The Gentleman's Guide to Cooking Through a Child Custody Battle* works.

The first thing to know about this book is that, as with my *The Gentleman's Guide to the Nasty Divorce,* which it is expected you have just read, what may appear here to be advice is not *legal* advice. I am not a lawyer. You need a lawyer. In the earlier book I suggest ways to find the right lawyer for you. It is assumed, for the purposes of this book, that you have done that. I will be suggesting to you where you want to drive the boat and how to get there. When you want to start the boat get the key from your lawyer.

For the purposes of this book I have also assumed that the new rental house has a stove, a microwave, some silverware, a couple of plates, soup bowls and glasses, maybe a spatula and that's about it. In order to prepare some of the dishes described in this book you'll need some other utensils, house wares and appliances. If you're out of the house now, your wife's probably getting the house in the Final Order, which will as a practical matter include the kitchen utensils. They're probably a throw-in. So, basically it's time for you to set up a new kitchen, at least with the things you'll need now and can throw in a box when you move. Okay. On the book's website www.gentlemansguidetodivorce.com I've placed a clickable appendix to this book where, chapter by chapter, you can find links to what you'll need to prepare the meals that are described on these pages. Look for it under "Survival Gear."

I've also given you the basics on bedtime storybooks, some movies kids like and even some music you can enjoy together, also on the website under "Survival Gear." To keep your kids, you're going to have not just to feed them and keep them entertained, but you will have to "parent" them too. There's a lot in this book about how to do that under the difficult circumstances of the moment, how to show off to the court what you have done in that respect, and the importance of doing that effectively.

Be assured there is not a single recipe anywhere in this book that any well-intentioned, literate, competent person cannot successfully complete. You may be surprised how well it goes. In this effort we are all helped by a strange quirk of human nature: seldom does anyone's home cooking taste better than our own.

On the weekends, and maybe Thursday nights too, the kids come over. No, we're not going out, except on special occasions like after the school play, or the game, or visiting Aunt Sarah. Going out because you can't go home is pathetic too. And being pathetic to the kids won't go. If you want to see your kids, Dad's house has *got* to be fun. In *The Gentleman's Guide to the Nasty Divorce* there's a chapter about how and why this is so, so I won't go into all that here. Suffice to say an essential part of making dad's house, or *any* house, welcoming is the food's got to be good.   And as for junk food, just a little here and there or you'll have the ex on your back. Trust me, she's getting regular reports from the kids – whether they mean to be reporting on you or not -- on every aspect of your program. And she's listening closely.

You could hire a cook to come in, and I did that once, but what does it really get you? Then the cook's the star of the show, and you've got a strange personality in the house when what you really want is to be hanging with your kids. We're going to get you an apron and a chef's hat and … if this is lemons, we're making sweet lemonade. We're cooking for the kids, even the little rascal who used to leave his plate untouched.

Here's the heart of it: you're in a fight and one of the disputed areas, one of the theaters of war, is the kitchen. Stick with me and we'll *out-cook the ex!* And her imported nanny too! (By the way if she doesn't let the nanny go ASAP, she's running way behind you right out of the blocks.) But that's just the start. Out-cooking her is the centerpiece of *out-maneuvering* her. Today is the first day of the future. If you've had a bad experience cooking before, if you think you can't do it, *try again … harder.* Because now the stakes are a lot higher. If you want to keep your kids, you can't afford *not* to do this.

You will also notice as you read this book that there is considerable emphasis placed upon kitchen safety. This is not because I am particularly safe in the kitchen, or anywhere else for that matter,

except in the field with a gun. It is because *you* should be! Why?
Because there is no piece of news – except maybe a DUI, or an
assault charge – that the ex would rather hear out of your corner than
that you almost burned your house down. Before the fire department
gets off the premises the ex will have heard about the fire from the
kids via their *i*phones, and her lawyer will have scheduled an
emergency hearing alleging unsafe living conditions for the children.

A custody battle is like pitching in the big leagues. Every time you
hang the curve, you pay. Of course so does she, the ex, on the other
side. The umpire in this game, for those readers who haven't read
The Gentleman's Guide to the Nasty Divorce, is the court-appointed
guardian *ad litem.* There's a lot in this book, as there is in the other,
about how to stay on her right side, and the importance of that.

Somewhere along the line your lawyer is sure to let up on the no girl
thing. Some of these guys are very cautious, however. It's not *him*
who's hitting the sack *alone* every night … speaking of feeling
pathetic. So let's just say your lawyer's still on his no girls jag, but
there's this nice girl you met and you feel like you'd like to get to
know her a little better. It's Tuesday night and the kids are solidly
with the ex. If you go out, by Murphy's Law you're going to be
seated two tables away from exactly the wrong person who's going
to yap all over town about who you were with. (These are the kinds
of jerks who come over to the table auspiciously "to say hello,"
which they have never done before, but in fact just to introduce
themselves to your ladyfriend so they can get her name and yap it all
over town.) You can't go out. You can't invite yourself over to her
place. So what's your alternative? There's only one. Invite her
over to the crib for dinner. Sure, you could order in. But a real meal
says she's special, and maybe she will be. Gotcha covered there too.

I wrote this book because I've been in just these spots – more times
than I care to recall -- and there wasn't a book like this to show me
the way. But with the help of a couple of friends – a good stainless
steel skillet, some dark brown sugar, vanilla extract, a rice steamer, a
crock pot and a tin of good olive oil for starters -- I found my way.

So will you.

<u>Forward -- *On Fun*</u>

I'm not sure if it's nature or nurture, but let's face it, most moms make it more fun for the kids around the house than do most dads. Okay, I said it. Maybe they just try harder. Moms do more huddling and cuddling. Moms shriek with joy when Junior comes home from school, and make a big fuss about the big hello. Moms go out and get the trinket that little Suzy loves, or the special toy car that Junior said he wanted. Dad never even heard Junior mention the car. He was on his phone telling someone to do something.

'Fun' is dangerous ground for dads to cede over, especially during a custody fight. The answer is not to start shrieking when the kids come in, although there's nothing in the world wrong with looking like you're glad to see them. The answer *is* to let the fun in your personality come out. A little goes a long way. What am I talking about? Here's an example. Get yourself a cooking uniform. It can be the double-breasted chef's coat and the toque-style hat. Or it can be a silly apron and a baseball cap. But get something that's you, that says you're cooking, and that by the way we're having fun. And wear it. Get a kid-sized one too, as an honor for sous-chefs who show enthusiasm.

These are tough times for sure. But there are big opportunities here too for dads to get to know their kids better – to focus on them for a change – and for kids to get to know their dads. When you've got the kids, you've got them to yourself. That's a great gift. No moping allowed. And no wasting time.

Here's what I mean. At the dinner table as you are sharing the fare, if you are able and inclined, make up fantastic tales about long-lost forefathers who cooked this dish and served it between Indian fights or pirate attacks. "My grandfather George's Uncle Cedric, the Mississippi riverboat gambler, learned how to make this gumbo when he was stuck down there in New Orleans flat broke with nothing but his six-shooter…."

Family history is a powerful elixir for kids, especially during tough times, because it provides them with a sense of their being a part of something larger than themselves. That sense, that feeling of being on a great team, is exactly what the best military units foster in their warriors. Why? To give them strength.

When it comes to talking about family, the actual facts are probably most nutritious when they are served with a dash of hyperbole, and the fantastic fictional romps make for delicious deserts. At the dinner table, take care to talk about the kids' days at school. The goal here is to get your kids excited, to make sure they are having fun, fun they will associate with you. Draw them out.   Let the ones that want to talk about themselves talk about themselves. Let the hunt and fish boys talk about hunting and fishing. Talk about what the kids want to talk about. But talk about their fabulous forbearers too. Because when you think about it, their fabulous forbearers are *them* too, the forbearers' blood is in *their* veins. And who else's? Well, *yours*. So who's on whose team here? You and the kids are on Annie Oakley's cousin Franny's team, and "Did I tell you about how Aunt Franny taught her kid cousin Annie the trick shot with which Miss Annie Oakley made her fame and fortune in Buffalo Bill's Wild West Show? The one where she shot through six playing cards lined up *sideways lying on their faces* with a .22 *from 30 yards,* knocking them one-by-one off the tabletop? Annie wanted Franny in the show too, she begged her to go, but Aunt Franny's pa, my grandfather's Uncle Clem, was crippled up and sick with gout, and Franny wouldn't leave him."

It's not just the food you want them wanting to come back for. It's the company, dad's company. It's being on dad's team.

Success is when, on his way up to bed, little Johnny says: "Daddy tell us some more about our Uncle Cedric the riverboat gambler." When you're having fun, they're having fun. And don't forget the goodnight kiss.

Cooking for the kids

BREAKFAST

Breakfast is a great place to start because it is where dads traditionally shine in the kitchen. No wonder. The short order cook dance is athletic and -- with sparks flying and smoke rising -- dramatic. The results come out fast. The crowd is waiting eagerly. It's quick and there's plenty of glory.

For their long-term health -- and to keep their parts running most smoothly -- kids should start breakfast with a little fruit. Half a banana, a bowl of berries, a sliced peach are all favorites. If the kids have been good, well half-good, you can throw a little sugar in with the berries or peaches. If you've got one who loves chocolate, and nine out of ten do, you can even dribble a pinstripe of chocolate syrup on the banana.

Remember, the point of all this is you want the little rascals to want to come back. When the guardian asks them, "How's it going at dad's house?" you want them to say, "We love it there!" If they say that, the guardian or the custody evaluator -- as the case may be -- will cut you in big on her recommended visitation schedule.

Cinnamon toast paste
Every kid loves cinnamon toast, and it's a breeze to make. Take a stick of butter and leave it out in a small mixing dish to soften.   If you're in a rush, you can get the same result by nuking a cold stick of butter for about 25 seconds (be sure it's covered in the microwave – these have been known to blow up). Add in 3 tablespoons of ground cinnamon and a cup of brown sugar (granulated sugar works fine too in a pinch). Mix vigorously with a fork, and then give the fork to the nearest kid for licking. Cover the paste and, to keep it soft and easily spreadable and meltable, cover it and leave it out on the kitchen counter while the kids are there. When their toast comes out of the toaster just spread on a thin coat of the cinnamon paste and let it melt.

If Suzy prefers her toast soft, no problem. Spread the cinnamon
paste on bread and then put it in a toaster oven or in the broiler until
the spread gets crusty. You've got a poor man's coffee cake.

When the kids go to the ex's, refrigerate the paste for use next week.

<u>5-minute eggs</u>

Fill a saucepan with hot water and put it on the stove over a high
heat. Pull the necessary number of eggs out of the fridge and place
them in the saucepan. If you wait until the water's boiling to put in
the eggs, they'll probably crack from the sudden temperature
change. When the eggs come to a full boil, set the kitchen timer for
5 minutes. When the timer alarm sounds, promptly spoon the eggs
out and into ice water. This sudden temperature change makes it
vastly easier to peel the eggs. Leave them in the ice water for ten
minutes. Then remove them and immediately crack them all over
until a fissure opens up. Begin peeling from there. A five-minute
egg should have a yolk that's a little gooey, but not enough to cause
a mess. Serve peeled, with salt.

Meanwhile, while all this is going on, put a couple of slices of bread
in the toaster. Spread cinnamon paste on the toast and bring it out
with the eggs.

If you have one or two 5-minute eggs left over, you're lucky. Put
them in the fridge and keep them handy for just-walked-in-the-
door/before homework snacks. My preference is with a pinch of salt
on each bite. Serve with a glass of milk.

As a general rule homework comes before play. This is tough on
dads because it means homework should be tackled, or at least
begun, during "work hours," that is before 6:00PM. And during
those hours dads, even if they're at home, are drawn to the
telephone. Resist this and sit with your kids when they need you for
their homework.

A winning line in the guardian's report to the judge in your case is:
"The children prefer doing their homework with the father." The

15

thing about school, like money, is it's easy for the court to assess the situation because it's quantifiable. The child's grades are either going up or going down or they're flat. Success in school is an important indicator of a child's well being, and the judge can judge it in a blink. In an arena filled with opinions, here are cold hard facts.

If you're the one they prefer to do their homework with, it is unlikely you'll be left out, especially if their grades are up. The effort you put in here pays big dividends.

<u>Chuckwagon-style scrambled eggs</u>
Some kids don't like boiled eggs, but they do like scrambled eggs. I had one like that who then grew up, so now he eats everything. But six-year-olds? Hey, there's just no telling. You have to pay attention, which means not listening to the words but actually silently observing and noting what goes in first, what gets snuck to the dog, and what's left on the plate.

If he balked on the 5-minute eggs, try him out on these.

2 tablespoons of light olive oil
3 eggs
¼ cup of milk
salt and pepper
Tabasco

Get the olive oil heating in the skillet over a medium flame, and swoosh it around.

Meanwhile crack the eggs and dump their contents into a mixing bowl. Add in the milk and a dash each of the salt and pepper. Stir vigorously, and then pour this "runny" mixture into the warm skillet. As the eggs cook they will begin to firm up around their edges. When about half of the egg is cooked and thus firmer, flip its two firmest sides in to the center with a spatula. Then pick up the whole and flip it. Let it cook until there is almost no "runny" egg left. If you have succeeded in keeping the whole folded and together as a single envelope sized piece you have just made a plain omelet. If it has come apart into pieces, that's fine too. This is scrambled eggs.

Scrambled eggs and omelets lose a little of their sweet taste if they are allowed to "brown," which is actually the milk getting seared. For this reason keep the heat a little lower than, say, for a steak.

Once you've got the hang of this you can play with it a lot. If the kid likes cheese, for example, grate some mild cheddar cheese and sprinkle it in before you fold the edges over. It'll melt inside. This is a cheese omelet. If in the cooking it loses its omelet form, just mix it around in the skillet with a fork or the spatula and it's scrambled eggs with cheese. He likes Mexican this week? Add in a couple drops of Tabasco.

<u>Uncle Sam's French toast</u>
The scrambled eggs batter that is approximately 2:1 eggs:milk is also French toast batter. Mix it in a flat-bottomed bowl, then immerse a single slice of bread in the batter. White bread's good, whole wheat's okay, cinnamon or cinnamon & raisin store-bought bread is better, and white from-the-bakery bread when it has been thickly sliced is the choice of many 9-year-old gourmets.

When the bread slice is soaked, flip it over and soak it again from the other side. Place the batter bowl next to the stove.

Heat 2 teaspoons of light olive oil in the skillet. When it starts to pop, place the saturated bread in the skillet. Then saturate a few more, depending upon how many mouths you're feeding. You can probably fit three pieces into the hot skillet at once. When the French toast shows a little light brown on the cooked side, flip it with the spatula. Put a serving plate in the oven on warm. Place the cooked pieces on the warming plate, and stay at it -- making sure you've got the skillet bottom fully coated with light olive oil before each batch -- until you've made what you need. If the kids have been good, or a least half good, lather a quick daub of your cinnamon paste between the pieces as you place them in the warmer.

Serve with maple syrup.

<u>On Triple-tracking</u>

You're a guy, so you can triple-track. You actually enjoy it. Let's take breakfast. You're (1) making the kids' breakfasts and (2) talking to them about their day. Who's going where, who's going to be there, and how they're going to get there and get back. On the third track you're making the cookies or the lemonade or the chili for later. Cook when you have the kids' company. Let them get to know you. It's pathetic to labor in solitude in the kitchen all afternoon. Don't make fun look like work. If you burn the cookies because at the crucial moment you were momentarily quadruple-tracking, that is to say you were unexpectedly down on all fours with your head in the back of the hall closet digging for Junior's soccer cleats, don't worry about it. Throw the sash over the sink open wide and pitch the whole rig, smoking cookie tin and all, out the window! Larimore the dog's out there. Let him be the first wave to attack the clean-up. Make it a show.

<u>Keep these handy around the stove</u>

There are several things that you'll find when you're in the groove that you'll need regularly. Make life simple and just keep this stuff on the counter next to the stovetop.

Soft butter: get yourself a butter dish with a lid and leave a stick of soft butter out. It will come in handy all the time, e.g. at breakfast for spreading on your English muffin, at lunch for making grilled cheese sandwiches, any time you've made popcorn, and a hundred other times. Cold butter's a pain, keep some of the room temperature stuff handy.

Cinnamon paste: This is a breakfast staple, although handy too when it comes time for bedtime snacks. Mix it up and keep it covered in a small Tupperware canister. Pull it out of the fridge and keep it handy when the kids show up.

Cup of salt: A carton of salt with the pour spout is very handy for extinguishing small stovetop fires. Keep that in the cupboard. But next to the stove a teacup with some kosher or sea salt in it is also very handy. When you need a pinch of salt to boil pasta, you've got it. When you need a pinch of salt to put on the egg you just pulled out for a snack, you've got it. Time to season up the burgers? The salt's right there.

Pepper grinder: Same as the salt. If you don't keep it handy, you'll be always looking for it.

Olive oil: Virtually everything you'll fry in the skillet you'll fry in olive oil. Get a 2 or 3 liter tin of "extra virgin" and keep it handy. You will use mostly this olive oil. But get a ½ liter bottle of "light" olive oil too, and keep it in the cupboard. Light olive oil doesn't carry with it the olive oil taste, so it comes in handy instead of butter in some circumstances. Olive oils don't need to be refrigerated unless you go away for the summer. Grocery stores sell lots of them.

Potholders: Keep two glove-style potholders handy. If you depend on kitchen towels to do what potholders do, you'll burn your towels up for sure. Both these items are typically available at the local grocery store.

Seasonings: We've talked about the need for cinnamon. The need for bay leaves will come soon. And there's more. You can pick these spices up one-by-one at the store, as you need them. Or you can get a kit containing the basics. Keep them in a cupboard near the stove.

<u>Personalized pancakes</u>

This is a fun variation on an American classic. Even the shy kids, who act like they're dying when somebody notices them, want to be noticed by their dad. Here's an easy way to make your kid feel special, because after all your kid *is* special. And if he's got a friend or two over, it's all the better. This proves you know their names.

a stick (¼ lb.) of butter
2 cups of Bisquick
1¼ cups of milk
3 eggs
a teaspoon of vanilla extract
3 heaping teaspoons of dark brown sugar
a small Baggie
maple syrup

You can make pancakes from scratch, but I prefer Bisquick-based pancakes to any scratch-made pancakes I've ever had. In fact it might be un-American not to use Bisquick for pancakes.

Crack the eggs and dump their contents into a mixing bowl. Add the milk and Bisquick and mix with a wisk. After a minute of wisking, take a break and add in the sugar and vanilla. Wisk for another minute and then set the mixture aside while you attend to the skillet.

I used to cook everything I cooked in the skillet with butter. Now I recommend olive oil. Why? My then-college-aged daughter got after me. She was, of course, concerned about her weight. And then my then-wife got after me because she said I was clogging my arteries (she really meant hers). So I converted for all things fried to olive oil and have grown generally accustomed to it. To me, however, pure olive oil doesn't cut it here. There's an exception to every rule and pancakes are my exception to the all-olive oil rule. For cooking pancakes, I cut light olive oil with butter.

To further bolster my case permit me to observe that my daughter, now out of college, who grew up on these pancakes cooked entirely in butter and requested them virtually every weekend she was a teen-ager is today trim, great, healthy (knock-knock-knock on wood) and she looks wonderful!

Slice off a half-inch of butter and melt it over a medium flame in the skillet. Add in a couple of tablespoons of light olive oil. Swish the mixture around the whole skillet bottom so the entire bottom is covered.

Now here comes the 'personalized' part. Pour a half-cup of pancake batter into the Baggie. Clip off one of the bottom corners about enough so you could pass a pencil through the hole. This is a poor man's pastry bag. If one of the little rascals who's in for breakfast is called Nelson, squeeze a *backwards* 'N' onto one side of the skillet about 2" high. If you've got another one named Sam, squeeze a backwards 'S' on the other side of the skillet. Let these letters cook for about 30 seconds. Then pour pancake batter over them the diameter of a squash ball, fully covering the letter. Let that cook another 45 seconds, or until you see bubbles bubbling through the newly-added batter, then flip with a spatula. You should see the 'N' and the 'S' clearly in the pancake's center. Remove from the skillet when both sides are a light brown.

After you've done a couple of these personalized jobs, give it up and step up production.

Pour in 3 daubs of the pancake mix making 3 saucers about the size of the previous ones. As they cook you'll see little bubbles rise to the top of the uncooked side. After you see a couple of these bubbles, flip that pancake. If that one doesn't fall apart, flip the others. The goal here, and it is very tough to attain through an entire batch, is that the pancakes will each be a golden brown on both sides. But if you fall short because you were a little impatient and used a little too much heat and the butter seared a little in the pan and the pancakes start coming out a darker brown, no one but you will notice.

Cook up all the batter in this way, for each skillet-full throwing in another half-inch of butter and whooshing it around the bottom of the skillet. Put a plate in the oven on "warm" and place the pancakes three-by-three on the warming plate as they come out of the skillet.

Serve with maple syrup, putting of course the 'N' pancake on top of Nelson's stack that you take care to show off before cutting. What you don't eat, freeze by threes in small Baggies. A three-stack of frozen pancakes is great nuked for about 60 seconds and served with maple syrup. With a half banana for starters and a glass of o.j. or apple cider, this is about the quickest and easiest kid breakfast there is, perfect for when the little slugger got up late, the Little League game starts at 9:00 and after an exhaustive search it is revealed the baseball uniform pants must still be fetched from the ex's because two days ago, when the kids pulled out, she forgot the pants were in the washing machine.

<u>Why kids get fat</u>
Some readers may have been alarmed that I suggested sneaking three heaping teaspoons of dark brown sugar into the kids' pancakes. In my view they should not be, and as evidence I present – right after I stop knocking on wood – my four children by three wives each of whom has grown up eating dark brown sugar snuck into their pancakes. As you read on you will find the brown sugar and vanilla melody reprised often and sometimes in surprising places. My children ate/eat all these recipes. May I also add – as I continue to knock on wood -- that none of my children take adderol, although one of their mothers ran a tough campaign to force feed the stuff to one of our sons as a way of getting his grades up. But we'll leave that unfortunate topic to another day. Nor finally -- still knocking – is any of my kids diabetic, although I have a family history of diabetes.

How do I explain their present leanness?
1. I never permitted television or video games on during the daylight hours – even on weekends! (Except Saturday mornings after games.)
2. I had a similar rule about computers. You can use them for school during the daylight hours, but not just for fooling around. And those computers are laptops on the kitchen or dining room or library table. Not hidden away somewhere between the sheets!
3. One last rule. If lunch or dinner is coming within two hours, no snacking allowed. If somebody looks bored, like they might snack just for something to do, give them a handful of raisins and kick them outside to play where they can climb a tree, or dig a hole, or make a fort, or go fishing or crabbing, or ride their bike, or make a snowman, or wrestle with their brother, or do any of the thousand things kids do outside. If they're out of the house, by definition they're out of the kitchen. In my kitchen, if I'm going to the trouble of preparing the chow, I certainly don't want to be seeking to serve it to customers who have ruined their appetites.

"But the ex lets them watch TV over at her place from the minute they come home until the lights go out," you may say. "If I tell them 'no-TV until dark' I'll have a revolt on my hands. They'll be boo-hooing not just to me, and the ex, but to the guardian too." Fair enough. Get smart and get there first. Talk to the guardian or custody evaluator about how much TV she thinks is proper. Tell her what you're willing to do. If she says an hour a night is acceptable, give them an hour. When you tell the guardian that the kids are vegging in front of the tube all day at the ex's, you raise TV-watching as an issue. Like who's helping the children with their homework, now TV-watching is another theater in the custody battle, and one where if you're smart, you'll gain an advantage.

<u>Good fats</u>

Among "healthy foods" olive oil is a champ. The primary fat in olive oil is monounsaturated fatty acid (MUFA). MUFAs and PUFAs (polyunsaturated fats) are considered by researchers the "good fats." (Saturated fats and transfats are the "bad fats.") Some of the health benefits attributed by researchers to the "good fats" are lower "bad" cholesterol and higher "good" cholesterol. Thus olive oil in the diet tends to decrease blood pressure and the risk of heart troubles. Olive oil also contains natural antioxidants that researchers say reduce cancer risks. In general, as well, it is a natural lubricant. The implication of that is that it keeps your moving parts running more smoothly together, handy examples of which are your skin which eating olive oil is said to help keep from drying out, and your joints which eating olive oil is said to help keep lubricated thus reducing the pain, for example, of arthritis.

If it sounds like only old people have to worry about all this, consider (1) that all these health risks are cumulative, and (2) good eating habits begun early don't require bad-habit-breaking later.

Omega-3 and Omega-6 fats (of the MUFA family) are known as "brain foods," meaning researchers say these fats -- that are found in cold water fish (and fish oil), walnuts and leafy vegetables -- are necessary for healthy brain development. Some expecting mothers take fish oil capsules for this purpose, hoping to get their kids an academic jump on their schoolmates. Brain development continues through adolescence. Trout is high in Omega-3 and Omega-6, which means you can go fly-fishing and make your kid smart too. Enlist his help in the program by taking him (or of course "her") along.

<u>Camo lemonade</u>

Keep a pitcher of this lemonade in the fridge at all times. Kids love it and in the evenings, or for that matter at any time, you can sneak a splash of bourbon into yours and no one, at least judging from the color, will know the difference. What's a whiskey sour?

Beware, know what you can handle here, and don't push it. Your lawyer will tell you no booze – period -- when the kids are with you. Teen-agers, especially the ones who grow up with parents who honor the cocktail hour tradition, recognize the scent of booze. Little guys? It's less likely.

The catch comes when something unexpected occurs, like the sudden visit to the emergency room because Jacqueline got a plastic bead stuck up her nose, or Jimbo needed 12 stitches after he fell down the tree house ladder hurrying in to supper. You've got to be at the hospital, and there's sure to be trouble if you don't look (a.) very concerned, (b.) cool and efficient, and (c.) *SOBER.*

2 cans of frozen lemonade
5 cans of tap water
3 heaping teaspoons of brown sugar

Pull out a big pitcher, put the two cans of frozen lemonade in it and then fill it with hot water. Leave it for ten minutes.

Pull out the cans. Pour out the water. Open up the cans and pour their contents into the pitcher. Add the tap water and the sugar. Stir vigorously and serve, or refrigerate for later.

The lemonade stand team can get $1/glass for these. They'll need a license to sell whiskey sours.

<u>On gathering</u>
Easily the most difficult and frustrating thing about cooking is going to the grocery store with a complete list and getting all the things you need back to the house in an efficient manner. The *gathering* part. Like a lawyer writing a brief, or a reporter getting the story straight, or a businessman getting the deal he wants, or a doctor nailing a diagnosis, the secret is *thorough attention to detail.* That means *sitting down in your kitchen with the recipe* and imagining all the steps that must be taken and the ingredients and tools that must be at hand to achieve success. Then you must look through the cupboards, the drawers and the fridge to confirm which pieces of the puzzle you already have and which must still be gathered. The pieces that must still be gathered must be committed to paper (or an *i*phone list) and that *grocery list* must be with you when you go to the grocery. Once in the grocery pay attention to what you're doing. Exercise patience and precision in making sure you have gotten everything on your list actually into the shopping cart, and when you have checked out make sure you have all your bags. The greatest risk to your cooking success is right here. It is in not getting off the blocks right.

Unless the grocery is right next door, you must also *plan menus* several meals ahead so that you have the things you need in the kitchen when you need them. Again, this means knowing what you will need to accomplish the task, knowing what you've got already, and having the rest on your grocery list. If you commit a little bit of the intensity you apply to other areas of your life to this task, you'll nail it. If you are cavalier about this gathering part, you will find the actual cooking part very frustrating. It will be like trying to take the test without having read the material.

If the kids are coming over for the weekend starting Thursday night, then go to the grocery Wednesday night after work. That means making up your list on Tuesday night or Wednesday morning. Part of it, like success in all things, is planning ahead. It is also being prepared for setbacks. In this regard, try to keep peanut butter, jelly and bread in the house.

When you can, take a child or children with you. One nice trick for keeping a kid involved at the grocery, and feeling grown-up too, is having a paper list and asking the child to read it off to you. When you put the item in the basket it's their job too to check it off the list. Now *she's* the manager, telling *you* what to do. Good, you're a team. Just remember what they say at the State Department, "Trust, but verify."

Most kids like to go to the store. They see it as a shopping trip for them where they can lay in their favorite cookies and so forth. Take them, and note what each kid likes. (Maybe sometimes the "big shop" for the weekend is Thursday night right after they get dropped off.) Then next weekend when one child is not able to go with you to the store you can still lay in her favorite. Also take note when the favorites don't get eaten. At that point take that child back to the store and see what he gets this time. Kids are fickle about their likes and dislikes. How else did Crazy Foam, or Mood Rocks, or hula-hoops make millions? It's okay. It's part of being a kid. Do what good moms do and pay attention to these details. Once you get the hang of it not only does it come easy, but it's very satisfying when you see your kid's eyes light up.

Your remembering what Johnny likes says to him you *heard* him, and kids – just like adults -- like to be heard. It says to them that they matter, just as ignoring them says they don't matter.

Before I forget, the Farmer's Market can be a great Saturday morning field trip. Chat up the farmers. Make it an event that can be discussed afterwards. On the topic of field trips, are there any races around? As a group boys love car, tractor, motorcycle, mud, and monster-truck competitions. Anything with lots of rpms. On the other hand the steeplechase and flat tracks are typically more preferable to little girls. Horse shows too. Few say they like the dog track, but they go anyway … for the people-watching ... once. Same with stockyards and car auctions. Go once. They'll talk about it for years. Be the one to open your kids' eyes wide. But play it smart and go when everybody's got a full tummy. Bring along some drinks and don't stay all day. Hit the trail long before the thing becomes a drag and the kids start whining to get out of there.

Auntie Em's grilled cheese sandwiches

Grilled cheese sandwiches are a staple for kids, but they are especially beloved by kids 2-10. At three-quarters of the little kid birthday parties you'll attend the hostess will serve grilled cheese sandwiches just like these.

Pre-packaged mild cheddar cheese paddies
White bread
Butter
Potato chips

Preheat the George Foreman Grill on medium heat.

With soft butter, butter one side of two pieces of bread. Put those sides out, making a sandwich of the two pieces. In the center of the sandwich put a cheddar cheese patty.

When the grill's hot put the sandwich in for 2 minutes. Then flip it for three minutes more, or until it's obviously toasted on both sides. You can make four sandwiches at a time in the grill.

Trim off the crusts, cut the sandwich in half and serve with a handful of potato chips and lemonade. I know, it bugs me too to remove the crusts. But with a grilled cheese sandwich the crusts become dry and brittle. Removing them makes a big difference to kids. Put them (the crusts!) in the birdfeeder and don't look back.

By the way, keep a birdfeeder outside the kitchen window and keep it full of birdseed. Also, keep a copy of Roger Tory Peterson's *Field Guide to Birds* handy. In the case of Peterson's classic, there's a book for east of the Rockies and another for west of the Rockies, depending of course on where you live. Get the kids into bird-watching and the guardian will *love* you. For your convenience I've provided links to these books in the "Survival Gear" section of www.thegentlemansguidetodivorce.com .

In addition to charming the guardian, getting smart about birds adds fun to the house. Something's going on. There's action. Plus, when kids learn stuff outside of school they can show it off in school.

What teacher, or flame, doesn't love the boy who offhandedly says:
"That's a female red-winged blackbird over there on the backstop.
See her stripes." In flameland that's as big as hitting a homer. Sure,
it's unlikely Junior will say to the flame, "My dad taught me that,"
or that he'll come home and say to you, "Hey Dad I saw a great
female red-winged blackbird at recess today. Thanks for showing
me those." But he's thinking it, and that's good.

Remember, if the little darlings don't want to come back, you're
going to see a lot less of them. When you're out of sight, you're out
of mind. And that's not just out of their minds, but you'll be out of
your mind too … because if they're with the ex all the time child
support's going up, up, up. Way too many guys pay all the money
and don't get any of the fun.

<u>Bush league hot dogs</u>

Little kids like hot dogs, and generally teenagers do too. You can
throw them in boiling water for three minutes. You can nuke them
for 90 seconds. You can grill them in the George Foreman Grill, or
you can pan-fry them in the skillet. My preference is pan-fried,
which is probably also the trickiest and messiest.

A pack of beef hot dogs
A pack of hot dog buns
Ketchup
Mustard
Sweet relish
Potato chips

Cover the grilling surface of the skillet with light olive oil, and leave
it on a medium-high heat until the oil begins to bubble. Put as many
dogs as you need into the hot skillet, watching out for splattering.
Cover. Give the skillet enough of a shake every minute or so such
that the dogs roll themselves over in there. Do this three or four
times over four minutes. Take a look and see if they look cooked on
their outsides. If they do, pull them off the heat. If not, give them
another minute.

Meanwhile in the George Foreman grill, toast the buns you need.

Pull the buns out, spread a daub of soft butter on the insides of the
buns, put the hot dogs in there too, and serve with potato chips.
Have some ketchup, mustard and sweet relish handy for garnishing.
If toasting the buns is too much trouble, serve the dogs ballpark
style, that is with the buns cold and straight out of the package.

<u>Roaring '20s egg creams</u>

You can make this now-nearly-forgotten refreshing drink -- that to a little kid is like ice cream -- with fizzy water in about 30 seconds. Even kids who don't like milk like egg creams.

Fizzy water
Milk
10 drops of vanilla extract
A tablespoon of brown sugar

Fill a tall glass 1/2 full with milk and top it off with fizzy water, also known as club soda or seltzer. Add in the vanilla (or a tablespoon of chocolate syrup for a chocolate egg creme) and the sugar and stir vigorously. Serve. Watch the ones with the sweet-tooth's drink the glass dry so they can get down to the un-dissolved sugar at the bottom.

By the way, this is a great and easy item to make in quantity for the Cub Scout dinner, or the church picnic. You *are* going to your church, mosque or synagogue aren't you? Guardians love churchgoers. And teaching Sunday school is worth huge extra credit with the guardian. Maybe Him too, but the reference here is to the guardian *ad litem.*

Exs love to sing a tune that goes like this: "Johnny called and says he's got a tummy-ache. The poor little guy. He had one just like it on Tuesday. I'll come right over to get him."

Oh no. Here again, this is dangerous territory to cede over. If you're in a custody fight, you don't want the guardian reporting "The only parent who can handle the kids when they get sick is the mother." The correct reply is: "No, don't bother, I got him covered. He doesn't have a temperature. He's in my bed watching Maxwell Smart, and I've got some chicken noodle soup here. I'll be here all day. If he gets worse I'll call you."

So what's the expanded first aid kit you'll need to keep around for "medical emergencies?" Here's the checklist, including the all-important first four items for protection against sunburn and its treatment:

A baseball cap
Sunblock, SBF 50, everywhere you go
A rash guard surfer's top for swimming & sun
Aloe
A variety pack of theme band-aids
Hydrogen Peroxide
Neosporin Crème
Children's Motrin
Children's NyQuil Cold & Cough
Children's Benadryl
Calamine lotion
Thermometer (top for kids, bottom for babies)
Tweezers
Needle & thread kit
Campbell's chicken noodle soup
Ginger ale
Gatorade
"Get Smart" 1st season DVD set

For aches and pains give him Motrin. For cuts and scrapes, it's wash with soap, daub dry, a shot of peroxide, a dab of Neosporin crème, a happy band-aid and a kiss. After removal with the tweezers and needle, it's the same routine for splinters. For minor burns, it's soap and water and Neosporin. Be gentle! If he's had the throw-ups, start him off with dry toast and ginger ale. If it's the trots, keep him away from fruits and give him Gatorade. If it's the sniffles, the problem's going to be at night when he can't sleep. Give him the NyQuil and tell him to sleep on his back with his head on a big pillow. If something itches, lather it in Calamine lotion and give him a shot of Benadryl. Be aware it may make him sleepy. If he's coming off a real bug, like he had a temperature, start him off with chicken noodle soup and ginger ale. If he's got any special stuff going on, like asthma for example, make sure you've got an inhaler with the right stuff in it and you know how to work it.

Put the pediatrician's number on speed dial and don't worry about calling up and asking a nurse what to do. Call the nurse *before* you call the ex, so that you can cite the nurse's sensible opinion when the ex starts in on all the dramatic measures that must be taken. If it's after hours, page the doc.

If it's a real emergency, get the child to the nearest emergency room, calling the pediatrician along the way. Worse, if you need an ambulance, call 911 and be aware that all 911 calls are taped. The dispatcher doesn't need to know how the accident occurred, only the current location and condition of the child. Keep your cool.

<u>The visitation diary</u>

Keep a diary on your computer that notes when which kids were with you and what you did. If a child felt sick and you called the doc, put it in the diary. When you went to the parent-teacher conference, put it in the diary. If Meggie had a friend over for the night, put it in the diary. When you went to Johnny's baseball game, put it in the diary. He got two hits? Put it in. When the ex calls to yak at you about your no-count life, put it in the diary. If you suspect she was into the *Blue Goose* before she made the call, put that in too. The diary is for your lawyer's use and may very well from time-to-time be shared with the guardian and the judge. Keep it short, confined to the facts at hand, easily understandable to anyone who reads it, and of course self-serving. Entries that are consistent with the visitation schedule that's in place at the time should appear in regular type. Anything that's going on that's off the schedule should appear in bold type. Confine the entries in this diary exclusively to children's issues, which includes, of course, any unusual news at all out of the ex's house. Be sure to note in the diary who told you each morsel of gossip so that later when a couple of pieces fit together, you can suggest to the guardian where she might go to get the story first-hand.

It is remarkable how patterns emerge from the nuggets in a written record that without it would be missed entirely. The ex gets in the bag on Tuesdays when she has the kids. She doesn't return calls on Friday evenings when the kids are with you. Sandra, your former next-door neighbor who works in the office with you and who still lives next door to the ex, happens to mention she's surprised at all the yelling over at the ex's on Sunday nights. "Do you suppose it's because Jimmy's so surly when he first returns to Kimmie's [the ex's] house?" she asks. Put it in the diary. When shared with the guardian at an opportune moment, all this is helpful.

Get into the habit of doing this. In terms of keeping your kids with you, it may be your best-spent time of all. "If a tree falls in the woods, and nobody hears it," as Marshall McLuhan used to say, "did it really fall?" Keep a record.

Exquisito guacamole

In a house with kids guacamole just disappears. It's a good thing, because it doesn't stay fresh looking long, maybe an hour. But it's easy to make and good for you. Bring it out before lunch or dinner with some tortilla chips, and if there's a one teenager in the house, the bowl will be empty in ten minutes.

By the way, if you can keep everybody's hands off it for the time it takes to cook a burger, guacamole's a terrific hamburger topping.

2 ripe avocados, peeled and pitted (save the pits)
1 tablespoon of lemon juice
½ cup of minced scallions
2 garlic cloves (crushed)
1 peeled and diced tomato
a pinch each of salt, pepper and chili powder
6 drops of Tabasco sauce
A bag of tortilla chips
Saran Wrap

Quarter the avocadoes, remove the pits and set them aside, then scoop out the meat. Place the avocado meat in a mortar and crush it with a pestle. You can also crush ripe avocados with a fork in a mixing bowl. Remove the crushed avocado to a mixing bowl. Add in the lemon juice, scallions, garlic, tomato and seasonings and mix vigorously. Then place the pits on top of the mixture, cover tightly with Saran Wrap, and leave it to blend for 15 minutes.

Serve with tortilla chips.

<u>The courtroom</u>
No, not *that* courtroom. A little jumpy, eh? Well … me too.

When there's more than one kid around the house there inevitably will be disputes among the children about who can use who's toys, whether Priscilla got a bigger slice than Sammy, who has to set the table this time, who's feeding the dog, and a hundred other things.

As the only adult on the scene, like it or not, you're the judge and jury. Keep these four principles in mind and you'll get out with your skin: "Split it 50/50," "Take Turns," "Flip a coin," and "If it's hers, then it's her call who plays with it." One or another of these principles will be applicable to virtually every dispute that arises.

Just one example, a favorite of mine. Let's say there are three kids in the kitchen and they all want the last brownie. You could draw from a deck of cards and the high card would take all, and maybe the winner would cut his favorite sibling in for a crumb. That would be fair, but there would still be hard feelings. Far better is to have the oldest kid divide the brownie into thirds, letting the youngest choose hers first, and the middle child choose his second. You want to see a brownie divided into equal thirds, try this.

<u>Tailgaters chili</u>

The day before the kids are expected, make up a pot of chili, especially if it's expected to be cold outside. Keep it covered in the fridge and when someone goes out early or comes in late, the chili's there for a quick off-the-schedule meal. Consider having some with a beer or two and *60 Minutes* Sunday night after you drop the kids back at the ex's. Then just freeze what's left.

Prep time: 30 minutes

2 ½ lbs of ground beef
1 onion, diced
2 cans of braised tomatoes
2 cans of red kidney beans
1 small can of tomato paste
1 red pepper, chopped
2 garlic cloves, crushed
1 packet of off-the-shelf chili seasoning
2 teaspoons Worcestershire sauce
2 teaspoons kosher salt
a cup of sour cream
Saltine crackers

In a skillet, the cooking surface of which is coated with 2 tablespoons of extra virgin olive oil, stir fry the onion and the ground beef on medium heat. Drain them in a colander and then transfer them to the slow cooker. Drain the tomatoes and put them in the pot. Drain the beans and put them in the pot. Remove the seeds from the red pepper, dice it and add it to the pot. Peel and crush the garlic and add it in too. Add the listed seasonings. Stir vigorously, cover, and cook on low for 10 hours. Serve with sour cream and Saltine crackers.

The key to cleaning up – besides the rock and roll track on the ipod - - is not putting it off. If you let dinner's remnants dry out in the skillet, you're going to have to scrub that skillet twice as hard. If you're in a rush, at least put the skillet and the plates in the sink, add some **dishwashing liquid** and run hot water over them, leaving the soapy water standing in them when you go.

Keep a few items around that make the tough jobs easier. **Steel wool**, dishwashing liquid, hot water and elbow grease will eventually get the dried eggs off the skillet. Don't use steel wool on anything but steel – like enamel for example – you'll scratch it. A step down from steel wool is an item that all grocery stores sell (by a couple of brand names) that looks like steel wool except it's made out of plastic. We'll call these **plastic scrubbing pads**. Keep a couple of them around for enamel cooking dishes and tough plates. Don't use steel wool on plates either, it scratches them. Then the next step down is the **kitchen sink brush** that has a handle and brush. Keep one of those handy for the easy jobs. Then you'll want a **dishrag** for wiping up counters and tables.

The dishwasher's kind of an enigmatic creature. You have to wash the dishes before you put them in the dishwasher. If you don't, the dishwasher will bake the leftover food onto the dishes and you'll be scraping it off with a knife. So get all the food and coffee rings and remnants of the meal off the dishes before you put them in the dishwasher. "Why use a dishwasher at all," you say, "if you have to wash the dishes before you put them in there?" Because the high heat's more sanitary, and it makes the dishes sparkle. Dishwashers take **dishwashing detergent** that is different from the above-cited dishwashing liquid. Dishwashing detergent comes as powder, thick liquid and in little cubes the size of ice cubes. The cubes are the easiest to deal with.

Be sure to keep the kitchen reasonably tidy when the kids are around. If you don't, one of the children will inevitably make an innocent joke about it within earshot of the ex, and she will bring it up to you and the guardian at the least opportune moment.

<u>Sea Island-style deviled eggs</u>

This WASP soul food is a forgotten favorite. For some reason deviled eggs say 'party.' If you have them around a house with teenagers, they disappear as fast as cookies.
Total time: 25 minutes

6 eggs
3 heaping teaspoonfuls of mayonnaise
2 heaping teaspoonfuls of ballpark mustard
salt and pepper

Boil the eggs for ten minutes, then remove them immediately to ice water for a ten minute cooling bath. Crack them all over, then carefully remove the shells. Halve the eggs lengthwise and remove the hardened yolks. In a mixing bowl crush the yolks thoroughly with a fork, and then add in the mayonnaise and the mustard. Season generously with salt and pepper and mix vigorously. Remove that mixture spoonful by spoonful, placing it spoonful by spoonful into the cavity in the hardened egg whites vacated recently by the yolks. If you've got some paprika handy, you can spice things up a little by putting a dash on the peak of the devil dressing of each egg, but it's certainly not necessary.

<u>School Snacks</u>

School snacks tell teachers what kind of fare your kids are receiving at home. So if you want Billy's teacher to conclude that when Billy's at your house he tries to survive on the munchies-style grub the pot-smokers leave behind, send Twinkies, powdered doughnuts, and Ring Dings in for Friday snacks. Oh, and the teachers will notice … especially if the ex has been sending in organic apples and boxes of raisins for the previous four days. The teacher will say to Billy something like "Ah, Ring-Dings again. Guess you were at dad's house last night." Unknowingly, your boy will answer truthfully, "Yes ma'am." Ouch! Convicted without a trial!

But that's just the beginning. The smart teachers (who after a few years on the job have already seen it all) will not hesitate to draw conclusions from what they see, conclusions you may not want to hear. It gets worse. Virtually inevitable is that you will see one or more of the children's teachers *on the witness stand* at a custody hearing.

That they may see their kids' teachers testifying under oath in their domestic case is, by the way, one of several very good reasons why, the visitation schedule de jour aside, good dads stay in touch with their children's' teachers about how the kids are doing academically, socially and psychologically.

Healthy snacks don't have to taste bad. Here are some good ones: Fruit-by-the-Foot, mozzarella sticks, Clementine oranges, apples, applesauce or yogurt in the snack-size containers (don't forget to send a plastic spoon), Nutri-grain bars, trail mix.

The best trick is to take the kids along to the grocery and let them pick out their own snacks. Just make sure they choose healthy stuff. That they are in the schoolyard seeing what their friends bring makes them experts on the latest trend. If the ex lets them run around like banshees when they go to the grocery with her, don't permit that. Just say, if you're not orderly in here, there's no Tootsie-Pop for you at check-out," and mean it.

Sweets as occasional incentives are highly effective. As school snacks they are lethal.

In the management of workers, and traditionally in the management of children, there are two alternatives: the carrot and the stick. In a custody battle, however, with respect to the management of the children, the stick must be put away. The choice is "carrot" or "no carrot." Thus the wise father keeps treats around, but under his tight control.

If you are stressing, go to the gym and wear yourself out slugging the punching bag. Some gym time is beneficial for a variety of good reasons that I have described in *The Gentleman's Guide to the Nasty Divorce.* You may strike the punching bag. You may NOT strike the children. You may NOT even kick the dog. If you do either, there is an excellent chance you will soon be marked way down for it by the guardian.

Lemonade stand-style tollhouse cookies

Every delicatessen and half the convenience stores in the USA sell chocolate chip cookies at the point of sale and not one of their recipes holds a candle to this classic, which you can prepare entirely while the children are in the kitchen for lunch. There's a great licking bowl here, and the way baking these cookies makes the house smell will bring in the neighborhood.

If the kids are doing a lemonade stand, they should sell these for $1 apiece. They'll make a fortune!

Prep Time: 10 minutes

2 ¼ cups of flour
1 teaspoon salt
1 teaspoon baking soda
2 sticks of soft butter
1½ cups of dark brown sugar
1 tablespoon of vanilla extract
3 eggs
12 oz. package of chocolate chips

Preheat oven to 375 degrees.

Mix the flour, salt and baking soda in a medium-sized bowl. Beat the butter, sugar and vanilla extract in a big bowl until they are creamy. Add the eggs one at a time, beating vigorously. Slowly beat in the flour mixture. At the very end gently stir in the chocolate chips.

Drop by rounded tablespoon-sized helpings onto un-greased cookie sheets. Bake for 8-10 minutes until golden brown.

Let the cookies cool on the sheets until firm. Then spatula them off into a bowl or cookie jar. Makes about 60 cookies.

<u>One-minute smoothies</u>

In airports they make preparing smoothies look like a big deal. It's not. You've got some berries in the fridge for the children's breakfasts? Here's a way to put them to good use in the afternoon. And just to be on the safe side, it's not a bad idea to keep some frozen berries in the freezer, in case you run out of the fresh ones. They work just as well and no one will have to go without a full portion.

¼ cup of orange or cranberry juice
½ cup of plain yogurt
½ cup of berries
a heaping teaspoon of dark brown sugar
a heaping teaspoon of honey

Place all the ingredients in a blender, cover, and turn it on high until they are smooth.
Serve in a tall glass. A tall straw dresses up a smoothie, but it's not necessary. If the smoothie is thick, a tall teaspoon can be very helpful.

If you've got a six-year-old who's tough to please, try her out on these.

<u>Mayhem marshmallows</u>

Here's the trick for that rainy Saturday when all the plans got wrecked by the weather. The kids are cooped up in the house and because they're bored, the big ones are picking fights with the little ones. You've seen tears, and you know there are more coming. What to do? Introduce two ingredients that are irresistible to kids: sugar and action.

Your first time out may well feel like mayhem in the kitchen with goopy stuff spilled on the countertops, confectioner's sugar splattered on the floor and on kids' clothes, and hardened sugar mustaches on kids' cheeks. Wear your long apron. I've gotten confectioner's sugar on the knees of my trousers making these marshmallows. Not to worry. It all comes off with warm water.

All these ingredients will last indefinitely, so buy them and hold them until the time is right. You'll know.

If you are going to use an electric mixer, you'll need at least one volunteer who can hold the mixer in a bowl for a few minutes at a time. An electric stand mixer will make it possible for you to do all that's required single-handedly. But if a volunteer or two are available, you bet they'll be volunteering because there's a big reward for them at the end: this is a first class licking bowl!

3 packages gelatin (unflavored)
1½ cups brown sugar
one dash of vanilla extract
1 cup corn syrup
¼ teaspoon salt
confectioner's sugar

Put the gelatin and ½ cup of cold water in an electric mixer bowl. Mix slowly.

Grind the brown sugar fine with a mortal and pestle. Put the corn syrup, the salt, and the ground sugar in a saucepan, add ½ cup of water and mix together over a medium flame until the sugar dissolves. Then put the heat on high and while stirring vigorously bring to a boil. Pull the syrup mixture off the heat.

Ease the syrup mixture into the electric mixer bowl with the gelatin and continue beating on low until the mixture is combined, add the vanilla and then gun the mixer up to high for 15-20 minutes, or until the mixture is a thick goo.

At this point you can add your own flair to the mix. If the kids like M&Ms, throw some in the goo and mix them in briefly. If they like chocolate, lace the mix with Hershey's syrup by hand at the very end. Or, in the morning after you have removed the marshmallows from the ceramic dish, but before you have cut them, gild the lily by spreading a layer of the children's favorite cake icing on the top.

Coat an 8"x12" ceramic baking dish with sifted confectioner's sugar, then pour in the goo. (Give the mixer bowl to the kids.) Smooth out the top and spread a thin coat of sifted confectioner's sugar on the top too. Then put the dish on top of the refrigerator or in some other out-of-the-way place overnight. Let it breathe.

The following morning turn the dish upside down on a platter. When the marshmallow cake falls out dust it some more with what's left of the sifted confectioner's sugar. Then cut it into squares and dust them with confectioner's sugar. Serve.

Charlie Brown pizza

You can buy a frozen pizza, and I've sure bought and served plenty of them.   Pizza makes a great kid dinner, especially in front of a special TV show like *Charlie Brown's Christmas, Lady & the Tramp, Robin Hood, Blazing Saddles, Cat Ballou,* the original *Parent Trap* with Haley Mills, or the NBA playoffs. But making your own is fun, easy, tasty, and theatrical enough to justify the extra couple minutes it takes to throw it together.

Prep time: 10 minutes

A bag of premade pizza dough
A bottle of pizza sauce (marinara spaghetti sauce will do in a pinch)
A pepperoni sausage
A bag of shredded mozzarella cheese
Salt and pepper

Preheat the oven to 425 degrees.

Lightly coat the cookie tin with light olive oil. Roll the dough into a ball. Then flatten it out into a big circle on the cookie tin. For those who are theatrically inclined -- there are some entertaining *You*Tube-style videos available online that amply illustrate this technique -- here's a chance to shine. Fold in the edges a bit to make them approximately twice as thick as the large center portion of the pie crust. Spread the tomato paste in a thin coat covering the center portion of the pie crust, but not on the folded edges.   Arrange the pepperoni slices on top of the sauce and then sprinkle a thin coat of the mozzarella over the entire area.

Other classic toppings, depending on the crowd's tastes, are as follows:
Fresh basil
Goat cheese
Halved canned artichoke hearts
Anchovies
Ground venison (browned)
Ground hamburger (browned)
Ground turkey (browned)
Sliced tomatoes

Diced onions
Halved olives
Fresh mushrooms (stir fried)
Canned mushrooms
Sliced red, yellow or green peppers (stir fried)
Sliced salami

Put the pizza in the oven and cook for 12-15 minutes (the thicker the crust, the longer the pizza will need to bake).

The recipe suggested here is quick, casual, bare bones and plenty good. But be advised: some enthusiasts make their own dough and sauce. Others insist on cooking on a "pizza stone," which is a handy item that can also be used for making breads, cookies and other pastries. As you get into this there are tons of ways to go.

One last trick kids love is "stuffing the crust." If you've got some mozzarella sticks in the fridge for the kids' school snacks, pull out four or five. Half them lengthwise and position them in a big circle on the crust around the pizza's perimeter, leaving a ½ inch of crust outside the mozzarella sticks. Then roll that ½ inch of crust back over the mozzarella sticks, encasing them in the crust. Some kids don't like pizza crusts because they say they're too dry and hard. Not these. The mozzarella sticks will melt inside the crust as it bakes and when the pizza is served the 'stuffed crust' will be the biggest hit of all.

You can cut your pizza with a knife, but a pizza cutter works best.

<u>Uncle Cedric's six-shooter gumbo</u>

There really was an Uncle Cedric. How can I prove it? This is his gumbo recipe. My sister Edie and I used to have it when we were kids. A bowl of Uncle C's gumbo over rice was dinner, a great dinner. We didn't want anything else … except maybe desert.

Prep time: 30 minutes

4 boneless chicken thighs
1 28oz. can of diced tomatoes
1 18oz. can of tomato paste
3 cups of chicken broth
5 cups of water
1 cup of raw onion, chopped
1 cup of raw red peppers, chopped
1/2 cup of all-purpose flour
2 cloves of garlic, minced
1 teaspoon of ground oregano
1/2 teaspoon of ground red pepper
1 bay leaf
1 tablespoon of celery salt
A few pinches of Cajun seasoning to taste
1½ cups of uncooked brown rice
a package of frozen okra
3 cups of thickly-sliced smoked sausage

Put everything but the rice, okra and sausage in the slow-cooker and stir it. Cover it and put the cooker on low for 5 hours. After the 5 hours, pull out the chicken and with two forks pull it apart into bite-sized pieces. Then put it back in the cooker. Add in the frozen okra, cover, and cook on low for two more hours. Then add in the sausage for 20 more minutes.

Shrimp goes great in gumbo too. If you have a couple of cups of uncooked shrimp, pull their heads and shells off and throw them in the pot when you throw in the chicken. If the shrimp you have is cooked already, add it when you add the sausage. Use the smaller US shrimp when you can. You don't want to know the conditions in which those gargantuan imported shrimp are raised!

Fish out the bay leaf and serve the rest over rice. What you don't use, freeze for later.

Uncle Ben's minute rice in a bag will work just fine. Way better is rice made in a rice cooker. These amazing devices that are somewhat recently on the market cook white rice, brown rice, wild rice, you-name-it rice and then keep it warm and fluffy all day and night. Just follow the directions that come with the cooker. If the family doesn't eat all the rice, freeze what's left over in meal-sized portions and nuke later as needed.

If you prefer noodles (a.k.a. pasta) to rice, they work just as well. And you don't need the rice cooker. Noodles freeze just as well as rice. Here's how you prepare noodles: Fill up a big pot with water and put it on high heat. While it's coming to a boil, throw in a big pinch of salt. Once the pot is fully boiling, throw in the pasta. Stir it so none of the noodles are sticking to the pot. After 5 minutes at a full boil, pull out a sample. Throw it at the wall. If it sticks, the pasta is ready. If it doesn't stick, keep the pot boiling. When you have determined the pasta is ready, pour it into a colander so the water will drain. Shake the colander a couple of times to get the last of the standing water out, and then serve.

Of these 'comfort food sides' couscous carries with it the fewest calories. Couscous is also probably the simplest of all to prepare. You boil it for a couple of minutes, cover it and set it aside. Follow the measuring instructions on the box.

Another word on safety: both the rice cooker and the slow cooker are designed to be left all day – and all night too. So if something comes up, you don't have to worry about getting home for them as you would for, say, your dog who needs to go out or else.

A word on the safe use of microwave ovens: Place food only in glass or ceramic dishes for cooking/warming in microwave ovens. Metal in the nuker -- anything more than a tiny piece or two of aluminum foil -- is a dramatic event that can produce what's known to the federal government's inspectors as "arcing," but which normal people would recognize as scary-sounding popping accompanied by sparks and smoke. Unless you want to see this light show, don't put any metal, including Chinese food canisters and plastic-coated metal "zip-ties" into microwave ovens. This applies also to china trimmed with metallic paint. Food wrapped in newspaper or paper bags can also be a fire hazard. Plastic bags, yogurt containers or cottage cheese tubs contain chemicals that can migrate into the food when cooked in a microwave oven. Yuk! In general, use containers that have stamped on them "Approved for microwave use." Also remember to cover these containers with an upside-down plate or another microwaveable covering when they are being used in the microwave. Do this because warming food can expand rapidly and splatter, necessitating a prompt cleaning of the microwave's inside. For this purpose, use a soft cloth or paper towel dampened with warm water. Do not use steel wool or for gracious sakes -- not that you would -- oven cleaner.

Swifty's chicken & biscuits

Here's what you want to serve when the kids have friends over for the night. Everybody loves it, and the moms won't believe you made it. Check this one out.

Prep time: 15 minutes

1 4 lb. rotisserie chicken cooked at the grocery store
1 package of frozen succotash
1 big can of condensed cream of mushroom soup
1 10-count tube of refrigerated biscuits

Pull the meat off the chicken in bite sized pieces and place the pieces in a big mixing bowl. Defrost the succotash in the microwave. Add the soup, the succotash, ¾ cup of water and pinches of salt, pepper, and basil to the chicken in the mixing bowl and stir. Then pour that mixture into a casserole and put it into a 400-degree oven to bake for 15 minutes.

When the timer goes off for the chicken mixture, pull it out and place the uncooked biscuits around on top of the chicken. Reset the timer for another 15 minutes, and put the casserole back in.

When the timer goes off again, pull the casserole out and let it cool for 15 minutes. Then serve family-style with a big spoon.

<u>Mediterranean vegetables</u>

The chicken and dumplings, and the following three meat entrees need vegetables to accompany them on the kids' plates. There are two ways to roast vegetables. Both cook in about 5 minutes. Master this. It will come in handy again and again, as every supper should include a vegetable. Broccoli, asparagus, Brussels sprouts, green beans, cauliflower, pea pods, and the sweet peppers (red and yellow) can all be cooked this way with great success.

Method 1: Spread the vegetables out on a cookie sheet, sprinkle them with extra virgin olive oil, add a little salt and pepper, and put them in the broiler for 2-3 minutes, until you see the first one singe. Pull them out and serve.

Method 2: Pour a big splash of extra virgin oil onto the cooking surface of the skillet and swoosh it around so the surface is fully coated. Over a medium high flame heat the olive oil until it starts to bubble. Spread the vegetables evenly in the hot skillet. Season them with salt and pepper and then cover. Shake the skillet once or twice in the first minute or two. Then flip the vegetables with a spatula and re-cover them.

When the vegetables start to look a bit withered, pull them off and serve.

More on kitchen safety: Hot olive oil in an open skillet can do some popping, especially if you toss into it something that's cold, and maybe has a few drops of cold water still on it. Watch your shirt and tie, if you're wearing one. If you neglect the skillet and it gets too hot, and you have a fire on your hands, pull the skillet off the flame and slap the lid on it. The idea's to cut off the oxygen, right? Here's where the old fashioned salt canister with the pour spout may come in handy. Pouring salt on a flame is a miraculous fire retardant. For bigger jobs, you'll need a fire extinguisher. If the house you're renting doesn't have one, get one.

None of this is anything to get wiggy about. Just be, as the Boy Scouts say, prepared. There are 365 million Americans today and 9 out of 10 of them are getting a home cooked meal tonight. Your odds of survival are impressive.

Alice's Restaurant venison spaghetti

When I'm at the deer processor I always ask for plenty of ground venison. This recipe is why. Here's a meal that's way healthier for the kids than a burger. It's cheaper, and it tastes way better. And I like a good burger….

Plus you can make it start to finish in the time it takes you to listen to the best folk song recorded yet in the English Language: Arlo Guthrie's *Alice's Restaurant*, which by the way is a song that, played in the car, fascinates kids.

Hamburger, ground turkey and even ground sausage can be substituted for the venison.

Prep time: 20 minutes

4 garlic cloves, crushed
1 onion, chopped
2 lbs. ground venison
a jar of store-bought marinara spaghetti sauce

Put 5 tablespoons of olive oil on the cooking surface of the skillet, covering it completely. Heat the olive oil over a medium high flame until it begins popping. Put in the garlic and stir it around. Let it simmer for a minute. Put in the onions and stir them around. Let them simmer for two minutes. Put in the chopped venison patting it down with a fork until it covers evenly the skillet's cooking surface. After two minutes flip the venison section-by-section with a spatula. As it breaks apart keep flipping it and patting it down until the venison is cooked throughout and loose in the pan. Then pour in the marinara sauce. Stir thoroughly and bring to a simmer. Then knock the heat down to 'Low' until you're ready to serve, stirring occasionally.

Serve over pasta.

Crock-pot dove

My approach is start the kids out on game, so they won't be afraid of it later. I understand the ex may view things differently, but show me a meat that's healthier to eat than a dove who's been flying free all his life and living off the land. You can't tell me a "genetically improved" chicken that's been trapped in a feedlot and fed chicken feed laced with growth hormones and antibiotics is healthier. I just don't buy it, and I won't if given a reasonable alternative.

You won't find dove at the local grocery, so it's going to be necessary either to shoot and breast the doves yourself, or to make an arrangement with a pal who hunts to get some of his or hers. If you have the opportunity to go to a dove hunt, by all means bring the children. The most fun is if you have a good retriever, your "bird boys" (or girls) can race the dog to make the retrieve. Every kid I know ages 5-12 has had an absolute blast being a bird boy, or girl, at least once.

Among game birds, dove is about the least "gamey," so this is a great way to ease kids into game. You can prepare this meal for the slow cooker with one hand while you're making your coffee and fixing the children's breakfast with the other.

If you can't lay your hands on 8 dove, 8 chicken breasts and/or legs will work too.

Prep time: 15 minutes

8 breasted and skinned dove (frozen's okay)
1 big onion, chopped
1 can of braised tomatoes
1 can of cream of mushroom soup
2 chopped garlic cloves
3 dashes of Tabasco sauce

Put the onions into the slow cooker. Pour the tomatoes on top of them. Put in the garlic and the Tabasco. Pour in the soup. Then arrange the dove in the mix. Turn the slow cooker on low. Put the lid on the pot. Good to go.

Come back in 8 hours. Serve over rice and with a vegetable.

Pineapple duck in the pot

There's hardly anything I like better than duck hunting, which for guys who are newly single is a way-more-cost-effective way to get your head straight than, say, going to a shrink. Seeing the volcano that is a sunrise while I'm out there participating in the food chain, and hearing all the sounds made by others doing the same thing … all that just shows me how small my part is in the cosmic drama. It's good for me to see that. So I have a lot of duck in the freezer.

On the subject of shrinks for a moment, it is a little-known fact that in a custody suit your shrink can be deposed and asked under oath by the ex's lawyers questions about your parenting style, and perhaps even what they know – what they have in their notes! -- about the details of specific incidents. Your shrinks can also be hauled into the courtroom to give direct testimony on the same issues. Included among the admissible questions is what they know about any extra-marital relationships you might have had. Do not assume some doctor-patient confidentiality canon is going to save you here. If you do, you are leaning on a weak reed. Talk to your lawyer about this … and about what the ex's shrink might know. Tell it to the sunrise. Ducks don't talk, especially the ones in the pot.

4 breasted wild ducks, skinned (frozen's fine)
a bottle of bbq sauce
2 tablespoons of olive oil
a can of pineapple chunks
1 small onion, chopped
1 small green pepper, sliced
2 garlic cloves, chopped

Put everything but the ducks, the olive oil, and the bbq sauce in a mixing bowl and mix it up.

Soak a paper towel with the olive oil and rub it around the inside of the crock pot covering the pot's bottom and sides with the oil. Arrange the duck breasts in the pot, and pour the bbq sauce over them. Then pour the contents of the mixing bowl over that.
Cover and cook on low for 8 hours. Serve with rice and a vegetable. Freeze what you don't eat in dinner-sized portions. It's even better nuked next week.

<u>Edie's chocolate cake</u>

Every kid likes a chocolate cake with chocolate icing. You can go to the store and get yourself a box of cake batter mix and a pre-made can of icing and you'll be just fine. Just follow the directions on the box. I've made plenty, and I'm sure I'll make some more. My opinion of the instant cakes is that the cakes are better than the icings however. And there's something a little creepy about that icing sitting on the shelf at the store year after year. I mean what's in it? Certainly not eggs, butter or milk.

So when you feel like stepping out, here's a cake recipe from my sister Edie that makes a super moist chocolate cake and a chocolate icing recipe that's over-the-top good. You can make it as a 15x10 sheet cake, or in 9" round pans, or cupcakes. Or use a mix for the cake and just make the icing here.

You will be a bona fide American hero if you take these cupcakes to your kid's class on his birthday.

Make the effort once. You'll be a believer.
Prep time: 15 minutes + 10 minutes

<u>For the cake</u>
1¾ cups flour
2 cups brown sugar
¾ cup cocoa
1½-teaspoon baking soda
1½-teaspoon baking powder
½ cup vegetable oil
1 cup buttermilk
3 eggs
2 teaspoons vanilla extract
1 cup boiling water

<u>For the icing</u>
½ cup butter, melted
4 tablespoons Hershey's cocoa
6 tablespoons buttermilk
16 ounces powdered sugar
1 teaspoon vanilla

To bake the cake pre-heat the oven to 350°. Coat the insides of the glass baking dish (for the sheet cake) or the tin 9" cake pans with vegetable oil and then flour. Throw all the ingredients except the water into a mixing bowl and beat with a hand held electric beater on high until it's thick. Then add the hot water and beat on medium for another minute. Pour the mixture into the dish or pans and bake for a half hour. Pass out the cake batter bowl for licking to whomever you've got handy who's been good.

To make the icing, melt the butter, and then add the buttermilk and cocoa. With a hand held electric beater mix it well while bringing the mixture to a boil. Take the mixture off the heat and pour it into a mixing bowl. Add the powdered sugar and vanilla and continue beating it until it's smooth.

Spread the icing on the cake with a knife, then pass the cherished icing bowl to helpers for licking.

Chris' popcorn

My friend Chris taught me all I know about the lost art of making popcorn. It's so simple, yet you rarely see it. Popcorn's great with kids before dinner, and probably best of all in its traditional use, on movie night. Now that online movie services have made it so easy to have movie night at home, let's make our own popcorn like Chris does. It's good for about 36 hours before it gets gummy, but between you and the kids it'll be gone long before that.

Making popcorn this way is so simple that parents who serve their children pre-packaged in a tin skillet popcorn must do so only because they haven't yet questioned the health implications of eating all the chemicals that go into processed foods. Chris' way is better tasting and better for you.

Prep time: 10 minutes

¼ in. of vegetable oil in the bottom of the pan
½ stick of butter
Several pinches of salt
½ jug (½ lb.) Orville Redenbacher's (hulless) white popping corn

Cover the bottom of a large (5+ quart) heavy-bottomed pan with vegetable oil. To be completely accurate my friend Chris uses safflower oil, a low-fat, low-smoke and high dollar vegetable oil. Over high heat, bring the oil to simmering. Pour in a couple of test kernels, keeping the heat on 'high." When they pop you know the oil's hot enough. Throw in the rest and cover.   Shake the pan vigorously and regularly. In about 3 minutes the corn will begin popping and within 5 minutes all that is going to pop will have popped. Take the pan off the heat and pour the popcorn into a large mixing bowl or bucket. Melt the butter and pour it over the popcorn. Throw in the salt and mix it all around.

Serve immediately.

<u>Aunt Sarah's popcorn balls</u>

Here's a really fun treat that you and – in particular -- your little girl can make together. Don't forget it on a rainy day when she has a friend over. Depending of course upon her age and focus, it may be she can make these almost all by herself with you just cheering her on. There's a lot of action here and not much mess. First, of course, you pop the popcorn.

½ cup granulated sugar
½ cup corn syrup
½ stick of butter
½ teaspoon of salt
8 cups of popped popcorn

Put everything but the popcorn in a large saucepan, mix it up, and bring the mixture to a simmer. Add in the popped popcorn and mix everything together with a big spoon until the popcorn is covered. Take the saucepan off the stove allowing it to cool for a few minutes. Fill a large bowl with ice-cold water. Put your hands in the ice water until they're chilly, then pick up a handful of the warm popcorn, rolling it into a ball and plopping it down quickly on wax paper until it cools.

Whatever mess there is comes right up with warm water. In a baggie popcorn balls make super school snacks, or at home for after school snacks. If they sit around too long and get stale, leave them out for the birds. That's where the boys get in the act. They'll love calling the play-by-play on the bird-fights.

<u>Bedtime stories</u>
There's a whole bunch of literature about all the ways reading to
children benefits them. And when you think about it, it makes sense.
Typically authors take more care with their words than parents and
siblings do around the house. So the word-smithing found in books
is better than the oral fare. If kids learn language by hearing it,
which they must because they can't read yet, then exposing them to
language that has been carefully crafted surely makes them better
language users.

There's no end to this, but here's a primer to get you started. Start
little one's off with nursery rhymes and funny songs and poems like
the one's you'll find in Kady MacDonald Denton's *A Child's
Treasury of Nursery Rhymes*. Then move them along to Dr. Seuss.
Much of his best work can be found in the anthology, *Your Favorite
Seuss*. Then move on to fairy tales like you'll find in Armand
Eisen's great illustrated *A Treasury of Children's Literature*. When
a child is about five-years-old you can start on non-fiction. A
wonderful series that my children have loved is Susan Wise Bauer's
The Story of the World. We read every page, but skipping around's
okay too. About now they can begin to read for themselves, but
even then, don't stop. Get them age-appropriate books from the
library and if their school sends books home with them, lay your
hands on them and read those titles to them too. Don't stop until
you've re-read for your own benefit as well as theirs first *Tom
Sawyer* and then *Huckleberry Finn*. There are links to these books
in the "Survival Gear" section of
<u>www.gentlemansguidetodivorce.com</u> .

Read to the children before naps. Read to them in front of fires in
the wintertime. Read to them at bedtime. When you can, sit next to
your child when you read to him, or lie on the bed together. Let her
snuggle up to you. There's something mysterious that happens here
that has to do with calm and trust and security. These are the
moments when your child is most likely to say unguarded things to
you. Here, in the safety of the den like a lioness and her cubs, is
where the little ones are internally wired to trust you the most.

Reading to kids isn't just literacy and entertainment, although it is certainly that. It's bonding.

Read to them whenever you can. And don't forget to have fun with the voices. Captain Hook growls. Peter Pan talks a mile a minute. And you'll need your falsetto to do justice to Tinker Bell.

This happens to every guy at least once. Everything's all set. The kids will be with the ex for Thanksgiving. You've made other unspecified plans. Everything's good and then you get the email, which of course is lies from top to bottom.

It goes something like this: "EB- My mother who was coming to Thanksgiving with the children has taken ill and I have to go and be with her. We're all very disappointed, and I'm very worried about Mother. I'll drop the children off on my way. It's supposed to get cold so make sure Johnny doesn't lose the nice new blue Patagonia fleece I just got him. Happy Thanksgiving! Laura"

Here's the translation: Her new boyfriend with the King Air has just gotten a last-minute invitation to a South Carolina shooting plantation to shoot ducks for the weekend, and she'd rather go along and party with him than spend all day in the kitchen cooking for her mother and the kids.

First off, and very importantly, you are not permitted to make any disparaging comments about the ex in front of the children. DO NOT, for example, CALL HER A LIAR to the children … even when she is lying. This is for two reasons. The first and most important one is children only have two parents and the blood of each parent, they somehow know, flows in their veins. Therefore, when you call the ex a liar you are saying to them that they have the blood of a liar flowing in their veins. This makes it easier for them to become comfortable with lying. So you are creating monsters. All the horrible things you say about the ex just give your children license to become horrible in those particular ways. That's obviously not good for them, and by the way it's *not good for you* to have horrible children. For starters it's definitely more expensive and much more stressful. Don't do it. The second reason is related to the first. Guardians know all this because in 'Guardian School' they are taught that it is Sin #1 to talk the ex down to the kids. Don't do it. The kids will tell and you'll pay. In fact, just don't talk the ex down to anyone. You don't have to defend her. But good manners dictate you not speak ill of her … even if you know she's horrible about you. Take the high road. The climate and the scenery are better, and the room's a lot bigger. Lest you forget, you at one time married her and chose her to be the mother of your children. Yes, that was you.

I know it was a mistake. Unfortunately it is a mistake that can be only partially corrected. It's best to make the best of it.

Okay. Gotcha covered on the holiday dinner. Making the best of it means having some fun with it. Families vary in size, but a holiday table should have some people around it. So if fewer than four children are coming, I'd suggest adding an "orphan" or two or three to the guest list. These would be family friends who don't have family dinners of their own to attend. Their extra hands will also no doubt come in handy serving and cleaning up.

At a holiday dinner it's always nice to stand up and give a little toast, especially if you're the host. Standard would be thanking the guests for coming and saying how delightful it is to be with the children who are so much of all that you are thankful for. From there you might work your way around to the beauty of the land, leaving them laughing by reciting Ogden Nash's *Song of the Open Road*, a four line poem that you can commit to memory in a minute and a half. It goes like this:

I think that I shall never see
A billboard lovely as a tree.
Indeed, unless the billboards fall
I'll never see a tree at all.

Or, of course, choose your own favorite.

What follows is an over-the-top holiday meal that you and the kids can make together and enjoy together all weekend long. So that it stages correctly, prepare it in the following order. Dinner's at 6:00PM.

<u>Floating island</u>

Floating Island is one of the most fun desserts the French have come up with. For some reason it's out of style. Maybe it's the calories, which I'm sure are over the top. But once you're up and running and enjoying yourself in the kitchen, this one's an amazing crowd-pleaser. Start it while you're cleaning up Thanksgiving Day lunch. This recipe serves six generously.

Prep time: 45 minutes

6 eggs, separated.
2 pinches of salt
1.5 teaspoons of vanilla extract
¾ cup of granulated sugar split 50-50
3 cups of whole milk
caramel syrup

Beat three of the egg whites with the salt and half of the sugar until they stiffen. These are the meringues.

Heat the milk until tiny bubbles form on the sides of the saucepan. Be very vigilant about this part – not too hot, and not too cool. But just right. By the heaping spoonful drop the meringues into the hot milk and let them cook for 3 minutes, stirring occasionally until the meringues are firm. Then take them out and set them aside. Take the milk off the heat.

While the milk is cooling beat together in a mixing bowl the remaining 3 eggs and 3 egg yolks, the rest of the sugar and the other pinch of salt. Pour this mixture into the top of a double boiler on heat, mix in the hot milk and as the whole mixture heats up, keep stirring it. Once it has thickened, pull it off and put it back in the mixing bowl. Mix in the vanilla. This is the custard upon which the meringue floats.

Pour the custard into a serving bowl, spread the meringues over it, cover it with wax paper and put it in the fridge until dinner. With respect to clean-up, both of these bowls, the egg whites and the meringue are a kid's dream.

When it's time for desert tonight use a ladle to serve the floating island into desert bowls. Criss-cross a little caramel syrup across the top of the meringue if you like, but it's not necessary, and serve for desert.

Okay, now that you've got the Floating Island in the fridge, take a break from cooking and have some fun. Throw the ball or shoot some clays with the boys. Take a walk with the girls. If the weather's lousy, don't fret. Pull out the backgammon board, or a deck of cards for a friendly game of Hearts, Go Fish or whatever else is the family game of choice. Go be dad.

Then two-and-a-half hours before you want to sit down (3:30 PM for a 6:00 PM) dinner, return to the kitchen and prepare the gravy, the stuffing, and the beans. There's some time in here for those who can triple-track to get the table set as well. If you have a daughter age 6 or up, solicit her help with the table setting and decorating the table and sideboard. Maybe she'd like to make place cards. At Easter decorate with colored eggs and chocolate bunnies, at Thanksgiving use gourds and feed corn, during the 'holiday season' use pine boughs and holly, if you have it handy, and to honor Independence Day use flags and firecrackers. To supplement the traditional, what's handy outside and/or in the garden? Got antlers? How about some shotgun shells? They're as colorful as Easter eggs. So are gummi bears and m&ms. Make it fun.

<u>Simple gravy</u>
It wouldn't be holiday fare without stuffing and gravy. But let's not make a Federal case out of it. Here's the easy way out. When you're at the store grab a package of gravy mix. Follow the directions on the package, which are probably add water and heat in a saucepan. Make it and then take it off the heat, but leave it in the pan for a quick re-heat right before dinner.

<u>Simon's stuffing</u>

Before you start thinking you can axe the stuffing from the menu, remember you really need it tomorrow for the hash. So hit the whole program -- you're the man, you're a legend: "Remember the year Dad made Thanksgiving?" -- and go ahead and put it together right along with the beans and gravy.

12 ozs. instant stuffing mix
1 tube of Jimmy Dean mild sausage
1 onion, chopped
2 cans of sliced mushrooms
3 stalks of celery, chopped
1 cup of chicken broth

Brown the ground sausage over a medium high heat. Leave the drippings in the skillet and pull the sausage out with a fork, putting it into a large mixing bowl. Brown the onion and the celery in the drippings. Pull them off and put them in the bowl along with the drippings. Throw in the stuffing mix, the mushrooms and the chicken broth and mix it all up.

Place the whole mix in a ceramic casserole or Pyrex baking dish, cover it, and put it in the oven at 350° for 35 minutes.

After you pull it out of the oven, cover it with tin foil and leave it on the stove to stay warm for dinner.

<u>Haricots verts</u>

Haricots verts (pronounced "Harry Covair" who sounds like he might have been a movie star) is just a fancy French word for what we know as baby green beans. Buy them fresh and keep them in the fridge until you cook them Mediterranean-style (for best and freshest results snap off a half inch on each end – recruit a volunteer for this) as suggested earlier on these pages. When they're cooked, cover them and keep them on the stove to stay warm while you attend to the turkeys.

Prep time for the gravy, stuffing and beans: 45 minutes

<u>Georgia Boy fried turkey</u>

If you haven't had one, these are the tastiest turkeys you'll ever eat. The differences from the traditional baked turkey are basically two: the fried turkey's meat is noticeably moister and the fried turkey's crunchy skin is a sweet pork rind-style treat that's all it's own.

Frying a turkey is *guy cooking* at it's best. It's to cooking what flat out in the bass boat is to fishing. First of all, you're outdoors, generally on bricks or dirt. The dogs are interested because the scents are irresistible. There's open fire. There's the rocket-engine roar of the propane jet. There's steam and smoke rising. Things go pop and splatter. There's a real danger of fire. And when the turkey's done and comes out of the pot the motion is pure *guy*. It is exactly like pulling a 15 lb. rabbit that's dripping hot oil out of a hat.

I hope none of that has scared you off. It is the truth and it was intended to intrigue you. Of course you have to exercise due caution. But make no mistake, thousands of guys are frying turkeys across the USA every day.

I had a carpenter working for me a couple of years ago who one Monday didn't show up for work. He was a good carpenter and we were finally getting to the end of the job. So I said to the contractor, "Where's Billy?"

"Oh," the contractor said. "Well now, yeah his girlfriend called me, he was out on the river over the weekend and the outboard motor ran out of gas. I reckon he'd had a couple of beers and he was smoking a cigarette while he was pouring the gas and the dang gas can blew up on him. You know that's a bad combination for rednecks, that beer and cigarettes and gas."

A couple of days later Billy was back on the job and he looked bad. No eyebrows or eyelashes and Vaseline smeared on where they used to be. But he had a big smile and he went right to work.

Of all those guys all across the country who are out there frying turkeys, every once in awhile there's a guy like Billy who gets hurt.

Don't let it be you. Instead see this opportunity for what it is: a great chance to hang outdoors with the kids one at a time where, like in a car, there's stuff going on to provide distraction when necessary, and white noise that provides just enough privacy for thoughtful talk.

1 10 lb. turkey
1 13-15 lb. turkey
3-5 gallons of peanut oil
6 onions, peeled
salt and pepper
2 cans of jellied cranberry sauce

Before you light up the jet burner put the larger turkey in the pot and fill the pot with water until the turkey is fully submerged. This is to mark with the water line how much peanut oil will be needed to fry the turkey. Pour out the water and, observing the water line, replace it with a like amount of peanut oil.

If store-bought turkeys are still frozen, bathe them in hot water enough to get the sacks of entrails out. I haven't had any trouble with frying partially-frozen turkeys. When they hit that hot oil they defrost themselves in a hurry. A decade or so ago my then-sister-in-law was appalled that I'd forgotten to pull the entrails sack out before I fried old Tom up. But then they all raved about how good he tasted. Not really a problem, but not particularly good form either.

Make certain first that the burner is on a level and sturdy footing. Then light it and put on the pot filled with the peanut oil. Clip the thermometer to the side of the pot with its tip into the oil, and cover. Let the peanut oil heat up to 350 degrees. At your convenience toss in three peeled onions.

Meanwhile in the kitchen make sure both turkeys are dry and rub them all over with salt and pepper. If you want to add garlic salt, or Worchester sauce, or rosemary to the rub, that's fine. Just don't use sugar or anything sugar-based, it burns.

When the peanut oil is at 350°, wearing a long-sleeved shirt and a cooking glove lower in the smaller turkey and fry it at 350° in accordance with the following formula: 3 minutes per pound plus 1 minute. Keep a close eye on the thermometer and adjust the burner as necessary to keep the temperature in the pot at 350°. Pull the smaller turkey out when the time's up, set it on a platter and take it into the kitchen to cool.

Bring the temperature in the pot back up to 350°, tossing in the other three onions, and then lower the second bird into the pot. Fry it in accordance with the same 3 minutes per pound plus 1 minute formula. When the time's up pull it out, place it on a platter and take it into the kitchen to cool for 20 minutes. Then carve both turkeys, putting the carved smaller turkey in a large covered mixing bowl into the fridge, and placing the carved larger turkey on a platter artfully arranged for your holiday dinner sideboard.

Serve with cranberry sauce, gravy, stuffing, and the haricots verts. Caution everyone to "save some room" for the Floating Island.

Enjoy! And don't forget the little toast.

<u>Ben Franklin's turkey hash</u>
Here's what you do with what's left of both turkeys tomorrow morning after breakfast. Select out a few of the best-looking slices of both the dark and light meat for sandwiches. Keep them covered in the fridge. Pick all the rest of the turkey off the bones, shred it into bite-sized pieces and put it in a cooking pan. Add in the leftover gravy and stuffing. If you've got a couple of cans of raw oysters in the cupboard, throw the entire contents of the cans in. Mix. If the mixture seems dry, add in enough water that it becomes moist, but not soupy. Put the mix in a 400 degree oven for 20 minutes. Serve with the leftover cranberry sauce.

<u>Susan's cold pea soup</u>

A country neighbor of mine invented this soup. It's lightning fast,
really tasty, and a great complement to the heaviness and spiciness
of the hash.

1-½ cups of buttermilk
1 package of frozen peas, still frozen
6 or 8 mint leaves

Put everything in the blender and turn it on High. When the soup is
the texture of a smoothie, shut off the blender and serve.

Cooking for ladyfriends

The bar's not exactly higher here; it's just got more booze on it. *And* this fare's got to be healthy-healthy-healthy, low fat/low carbs-sounding because women are always watching their waistlines … and we guys want them to. So it's going to be no butter, modest portions, and blueberries for desert. You yourself may or may not wish to walk the walk entirely, but you can at least talk the talk. Here are the basics.

As a group women are legitimately very concerned about breast cancer. They have got the olive oil antioxidant message, and along with it have absorbed the scientific research that says fruits and vegetables are high in vitamins that strengthen the immune system, especially against carcinogens. These are typically the bright-colored fruits and vegetables with broccoli, red, orange and yellow peppers, blueberries and mangoes being among the all-stars. Seafood, especially oysters, are also big hitters on the antioxidant team.

Oysters are rock stars. Don't forget them. They are very high in zinc, which builds bone strength thus helping combat osteoporosis, a condition that particularly concerns women. And, oysters are uniquely high in testosterone which researchers say helps prevent prostate cancer and – by the way – increases sexual function in both men and women, although, as it is said, cumulatively not immediately.

Miraculously there's a ton of research that says wine is good for you, particularly red wine. Red wine contains antioxidants and resveratrol, which means it's good for your immune system and your circulatory system. Simply put, the word on the street is red wine helps prevent heart attacks, strokes and cancer. So we're going to keep plenty of Argentinean malbecs and French medocs handy.

Recent studies have shown white wine is good for the lungs and circulatory system too. So lay in some modest French Pouilly-Fuisse's and California pinot grigios. Moreover, many women prefer white wine simply because it is said a glass of white contains fewer calories than a glass of red.

There are links to these wines in the "Survival Gear" section of this book's website, www.gentlemansguidetodivorce.com .

If you use these ingredients you won't go wrong, at least on the health front.

Now, with the basics of the requisite rhetoric in hand, you can move on to the cooking, which may or may not be consistent with the rhetoric. But it is, as are hopefully some of these early sleepover companions, uncomplicated, fun, fast and good.

HORS-D'OEUVRES

Oysters tapa

1 10 oz. can of oysters
1 tablespoon of white wine vinegar

Drain the clams and put them in a soup bowl. Add in the vinegar and a couple of pinches of salt and mix it up.

Eat them with a fork, or go one better and get a roll of French bread, the tube-shaped bread with the hard crust. Crack off pieces by hand, spread a daub of Philadelphia crème cheese on the bread and then put a couple of oysters on that. Eat with your fingers.

Once you've got the bread and crème cheese, you can move up.

<h1 style="text-align:center"><u>Smoked salmon</u></h1>

¼ lb of smoked salmon, sliced
small bottle of capers
small onion, chopped
1 lemon, halved

Crack off a piece of bread, spread on the daub of crème cheese, fold a piece of salmon onto the crème cheese, and add a couple of capers and a pinch of the onions. Then squeeze on a couple of drips of the lemon juice. Eat with your fingers.

It's always nice to share a little cocktail in the kitchen while you're fixing up dinner. To begin put 4 stemmed martini glasses in the freezer.

If wine's good for you, real booze must be even better. It's just the researchers haven't discovered how yet. Of the hard stuff women prefer vodka because its reputation is it has fewer calories than the others.

I'm going to go out on a limb here because women are very complicated and stereotyping is not only risky, it's impossible. So consider the following theory as just a way of narrowing down options by playing the odds. If she's wearing gold, silver or pastels offer her a Cosmo first. If she's wearing earth tones, lead with the Dirty martini. And, as always, be prepared to be completely wrong and graceful about it.

The Cosmopolitan, a.k.a. "Cosmo"

This cocktail, which was popularized by the television show *Sex in the City,* is characterized by its ladylike pink hue. Well made, a Cosmo is anything but exclusively a lady's cocktail, however.

2 jiggers of good vodka
1 jigger of the juice of a freshly squeezed lime
1 jigger of unsweetened cranberry juice
½ jigger of Cointreau
two twists of lime

Put everything but the lime twist in a cocktail shaker with some ice and shake it vigorously. Leave the ice in the shaker and pour the

Cosmos equally into two refrigerated stemmed cocktail glasses. Add
in the lime twists and serve immediately.

The emergence of *You*Tube has brought the art of cocktail-shaking
out of the shadows and onto your *i*pad. If there are a dozen ways to
shake a cocktail shaker, all twelve are there

<u>The Dirty Martini</u>

Because they were a favorite during Prohibition when they were
made with bathtub gin, Martinis are classically glamorous. Zelda
and Scott Fitzgerald are said to have favored them in their Paris
years. Winston Churchill is known to have had very exact
specifications for his favored cocktail (ice cold gin and an olive, hold
the vermouth and the olive juice). In its most recent incarnation,
however, the "dirty" (that is to say with olive juice) variation is
widely favored, especially by ladies.

2 jiggers of gin (or vodka)
4 drops of dry vermouth
2 tiny splashes of the olive juice from the olive jar
two olives

Put everything but the olives in a cocktail shaker with some ice and
shake it vigorously.

Leave the ice in the shaker and pour the Martinis equally into two
refrigerated stemmed cocktail glasses. Add in the olives and serve
immediately.

Coq au vin

This is a Burgundian classic that means "cock cooked in wine," and it is a great French delicacy. She won't believe it, because unless you use this braising base it takes all day to make coq au vin. Nobody makes this at home.
Prep time 20 minutes

1 jar of Williams-Sonoma coq au vin braising base
2 lbs. of boneless chicken, chopped and browned in olive oil
½ cup of pearl onions
1 bay leaf
2 tsp. of brown sugar
½ stick of soft butter
½ cup of red wine

Brown the chicken in a skillet over olive oil. Then brown the onions too. Place the braising base, the chicken, the onions, the bay leaf, the sugar, the butter, and salt and pepper to taste in the slow cooker. Stir and cook on high for 45 minutes. Add the wine, turn the heat to low, and cook for 15 minutes more.

Serve with couscous, a Mediterranean vegetable and red wine.

<u>Oysters in white wine</u>

This one's classic Mediterranean fare, perfectly consistent with the rhetoric, and a real treat.   If you love clams and/or mussels, and you have some freshly picked and in the shell handy, throw them in when you throw in the oysters. You may wish to brown scallops and/or shrimp and add them in too.

Prep time: 15 minutes

2 tablespoons extra virgin olive oil
1 onion, chopped
2 garlic cloves, crushed
1 teaspoon of flour
½ cup white wine
1 bay leaf
2 tablespoons of fresh lemon juice
2 dozen raw oysters

Heat the olive oil to simmering in a shallow casserole. Add in the onion and garlic and mix them around in the hot oil until the onion is wilted. Continuing to mix, add in the flour, and stir until smooth. Add in the bay leaf, wine and lemon juice. Add salt and pepper to taste. Cover and simmer for 5 minutes. Then add in the oysters and cover until the oysters open.

Remove the bay leaf and serve with a Mediterranean vegetable and white wine.

<u>Steak au poive</u>

With this French bistro classic there's plenty of drama, as you and your ladyfriend will soon see, especially if you permit her to get involved in the production.

Prep time: 15 minutes

2 New York strip steaks
2½ teaspoons of coarsely ground black pepper
the juice of a lemon
2 jiggers of cognac
¼ cup heavy cream
½ stick of butter

Place the steaks on a cutting board, distribute the pepper evenly over them and with the heel of your hand press the pepper hard into the meat.

Put a thin coat of salt on the bottom of a skillet on high heat. When the salt begins to brown put the steaks on. Cook for three minutes on one side and two on the other. Right at the end of the second side pour a jigger of cognac on the steaks. (Here you might ask your friend to pour on the cognac.) Leave it for a moment and then ignite it. Stand back.

When the flames die down remove the steaks to a platter and let the skillet cool for a moment. Place the butter in the cooling skillet first and wait until it melts. Then over a medium heat add in the cream, the remaining jigger of cognac, and the lemon juice. Stir this mixture up and bring it to a low boil. Then pour it 50/50 over the steaks. As it cools it also thickens, so a small pitcher of extra sauce on the table will not be out of place.

Serve with noodles (the French prefer 'frites,' which are essentially French fries) a Mediterranean vegetable and plenty of red wine.

<u>**BREAKFAST**</u>

While you're ordering the coq au vin from Williams-Sonoma, get a couple of boxes of their frozen breakfast pastries too and just put them in the back of the freezer for special occasions. The dinner omelet will also serve well for breakfast here, if you've got the time. Whatever you're serving be gracious and unhurried. This meal is, of course, unplanned, as you never expected that she would stay over. Serve with some berries, coffee and juice, and you'll be just fine.

<u>What now?</u>
In all the commotion you might not have noticed it, but you can cook! It's time to move up. The kids and you are getting spoiled. Not to mention, of course, the ladyfriends. Go out and get yourself a real cookbook. You've earned it.

Oh, and one last thing. You got the rules from me, your lawyer and the guardian or custody evaluator. And as you played the miserable game you tried your best to follow them. To you it was "Here's what I've got to do to stay critically involved in the raising of my children." But something else happened that you hardly noticed. Along the way you became accustomed to reading to your children at bedtime, to telling them stories, to watching what they eat, to washing their clothes when it was necessary, to sitting with them while they did their homework, to getting to know their friends, to staying up with their teachers, to patching them up when they fell, to hearing them when they spoke to you, to settling fairly their disputes, and to giving faithfully of good-night kisses. Along the way you came to know their fears and their dreams. Having to parent solo, you became a better dad. And there's a lot of reward for that for a long time.

Equivalent measures

3 teaspoons = 1 tablespoon
4 tablespoons = ¼ cup
5 tablespoons + 1 teaspoon =1/3 cup
12 tablespoons = ¾ cup
16 tablespoons = 1 cup
2 tablespoons = 1 fl. ounce
1 jigger = 1.5 fl. ounces = 3 tablespoons
2 cups = 16 fl. ounces = 1 pint
2 pints = 1 quart
4 quarts = 1 gallon
1 lb. = 16 ozs.
1 lb. of butter = 4 sticks
1 lb. of brown sugar = 2 ¼ cups well packed
1 lb. of granulated sugar = 2 cups
1 cup uncooked rice = 3 cups cooked rice
3 tablespoons of lemon juice = the juice of 1 lemon

Bake: Cook in oven.
Beat: Mix ingredients vigorously until smooth.
Boil: Heat until bubbles rise continuously.
Broil: Cooked by high heat supplied solely from above.
Brown: Fry on high heat in the skillet over olive oil until the edges are brown.
Chop: Cut into fingertip-sized pieces.
Dice: Cut into cubes smaller than 1/2 inch across.
Grate: Slice in a grater into tiny particles.
Marinate: Immersing food in a savory liquid for several hours, usually to tenderize meat.
Mix: Combining elements so that they are equally distributed.
Pinch: The amount that you can hold between your thumb and index finger.
Rub: Seasonings rubbed onto meat before the meat is cooked.
Simmer: Heat until tiny bubbles begin to creep up the sides of the saucepan.
Twist: A thin slice of rind a little bigger than a postage stamp.

<u>Acknowledgements</u>

This book is mostly about all-American kid cuisine. Cooking for my children and their friends has made me the cook – good or bad – that I am. It's easy in the rush of events to take for granted the seemingly commonplace moments that are family meals … until the era has passed. In the relative calm of that later time, one comes to see clearly the glory of one's children's daily company and upbringing, and the primal value to the soul of hunting and gathering for them. Sometimes the hours seem long, the emotional stuff withering and the price high, but remuneration in the gold of children's smiles and laughter, and finally their returned loyalty, makes it all easily worth it. To my children, all-American kids all, thanks for being great.

Sharing meals and ideas are two of life's great pleasures, and when the two are combined the experience can be sublime. I am lucky to have some great friends and entertaining family with whom I am privileged to regularly share meals and thoughts. Some of them positively love to eat. Others feel the same way about talking. From some of them and the meals we have shared, some of the ideas and recipes in this book emerged. In those instances I have attached the inspirer's name to the title of the recipe that they inspired. Salute.

Thanks to Ogden Nash for writing *The Song of the Open Road,* and to The Grateful Dead for bringing us *Uncle John's Band.*

Grateful thanks also to my editor, A.B., who has a keen ear for the music of language, a sharp eye for precision of expression, and an uncanny sense of how the parts of a book best fit together to make up the whole. This book is much better for A.B.'s involvement. Thanks Andy.

Most of all this entire project owes its greatest debt to my best pal, S.S., who has offered me thoughtful encouragement throughout all of it, and who has contributed in one way or another to every aspect of it from the project's conception to the writing and aggregation of both books, to the details of and launch of the website and beyond. From me, and all the guys who have been and will be helped through a rough time by the *Gentleman's Guide* project, a big Thank You goes to S.S.

-

EBG

For more, visit the clubhouse at:

gentlemansguidetodivorce.com